MINDFULNESS ON THE

PLAYGROUND

PRISCILLA AN

childsworld.com

The Child's World®
childsworld.com

Published by The Child's World®
800-599-READ · www.childsworld.com

Photography Credits
Photographs ©: iStockphoto, cover, 1, 15, 16, 19, 20; Patryk Kosmider/Shutterstock Images, 3; Shutterstock Images, 4–5, 6–7, 9, 11, 12–13; Zoteva/Shutterstock Images, 22

ISBN Information
9781503869585 (Reinforced Library Binding)
9781503880894 (Portable Document Format)
9781503882201 (Online Multi-user eBook)
9781503883512 (Electronic Publication)
9781645498643 (Paperback)

LCCN 2022951169

Printed in the United States of America

Priscilla An is a children's book editor and author. She lives in Minnesota with her rabbit and likes to practice mindfulness through yoga.

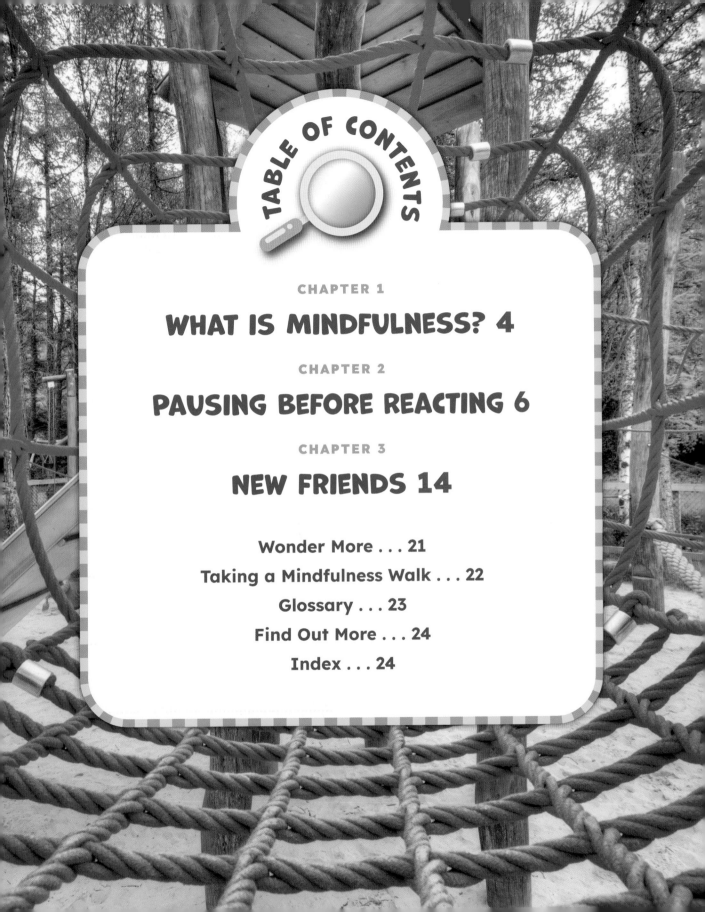

TABLE OF CONTENTS

WHAT IS MINDFULNESS?

People can sometimes face struggles on the playground. Friends may not be nice. It might be hard to **approach** new people and ask to play with them. Practicing mindfulness can help. Mindfulness is when people pay attention to their thoughts, feelings, and surroundings. Being mindful can help people pause when they are angry. It can help people find the courage to make new friends.

The playground is a great place to practice mindfulness.

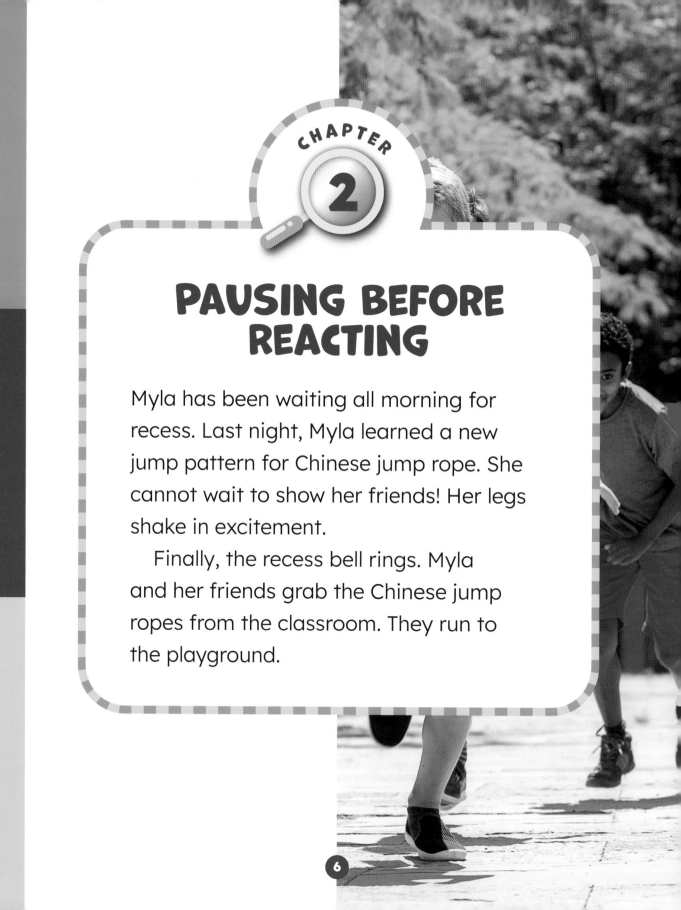

PAUSING BEFORE REACTING

Myla has been waiting all morning for recess. Last night, Myla learned a new jump pattern for Chinese jump rope. She cannot wait to show her friends! Her legs shake in excitement.

Finally, the recess bell rings. Myla and her friends grab the Chinese jump ropes from the classroom. They run to the playground.

Recess is a fun break from studying.

Myla is first in line. She prepares to run and jump in the middle of the ropes. But Jessica pushes Myla aside and starts jumping.

"Hey, I was first!" Myla says.

"Oops, I didn't see you!" Jessica laughs.

As Jessica jumps, James walks over to Myla. "I hope she gives the rest of us a chance to go," he whispers. "Last time she cut in line, too."

Myla feels like she is going to explode. Sometimes Jessica only thinks about herself! Myla makes a fist with her hands. Maybe she can teach Jessica a lesson. She can push Jessica just like *she* pushed *her*.

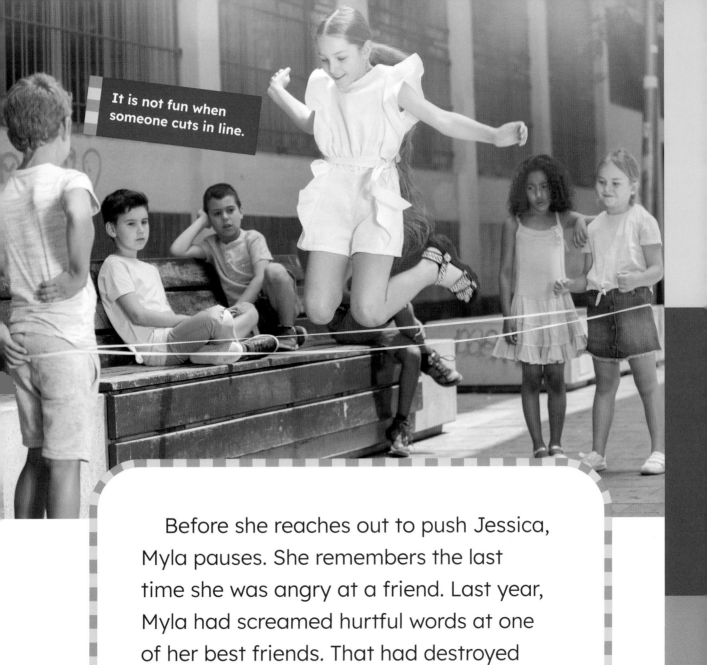

It is not fun when someone cuts in line.

Before she reaches out to push Jessica, Myla pauses. She remembers the last time she was angry at a friend. Last year, Myla had screamed hurtful words at one of her best friends. That had destroyed their friendship.

Myla **regrets** what she did to that friend. She has thought a lot about how she could have **resolved** that **conflict**. She wishes she had spoken calmly to her friend.

Myla unclenches her fists. Jessica is one of her closest friends. Myla does not want to hurt her, too. But she wants to tell Jessica that her actions are not right. Myla decides to gather her friends together.

"Hey guys," she says. "Can we talk?"

Myla reminds Jessica and her friends about the line. She tells them that it would be fair if everyone got a turn.

Talking to your friends about your feelings can be healthy.

STAYING CALM

Anger is not a bad emotion. But when people react in anger without thinking, they can make mistakes. For example, they can say things they do not mean. They can hurt the people around them. Simple actions such as counting to ten before speaking or writing in a journal can help people stay calm.

Friendships can be saved through apologies.

After talking to her friends, Myla turns to Jessica. Myla explains that she was so excited to play Chinese jump rope. She felt angry that Jessica cut in line. Myla also felt hurt that Jessica was not thinking about her.

"I'm sorry," Jessica says. "I should have thought about you and everyone else."

"Thank you for apologizing. I **forgive** you," Myla says. "Let's go play!" Myla smiles at Jessica. They both run and jump rope again. Myla is glad she paused and thought about her anger. Practicing mindfulness helped her feel calm before speaking to Jessica. She was able to express her anger in a healthy way.

CHAPTER 3

NEW FRIENDS

Noah is starting at a new school. He is nervous about making friends. The kids in his class already know each other. After lunch, everyone runs to the playground. He hopes to make new friends there.

Noah watches a group of kids. They are planning to play hide-and-seek. Noah wants to join. But he is nervous about introducing himself.

Being in a new place can be tough.

Making new friends takes courage.

16

Noah starts to walk toward the group. But he feels **overwhelmed**. He is scared that the kids will **reject** him. He goes to the swings instead. Noah had a lot of friends at his old school. They all knew each other well. He never had to worry about making friends.

As Noah swings, his heart beats faster. Sweat starts to trickle down his face. Maybe he can try to make new friends tomorrow. He is comfortable being on the swings by himself. He tries to imagine himself walking over to the group. What if they ignore him? What if he says the wrong thing?

Noah shakes his head. Instead of worrying more, he **focuses** on how his body feels as he swings. Noah feels the breeze on his face. His body feels light. He breathes in deeply. Noah realizes that worrying about the future does not help. Maybe the kids are nice and will not reject him. He will not know unless he introduces himself.

Noah gets off the swings and walks to the group. "Hi, I'm Noah. Can I play with you guys?" Noah asks. He is still nervous. But he feels more hopeful.

"Of course! My name is Cindy," the girl says. "That's Mason, Ethan, and Liam." The boys wave.

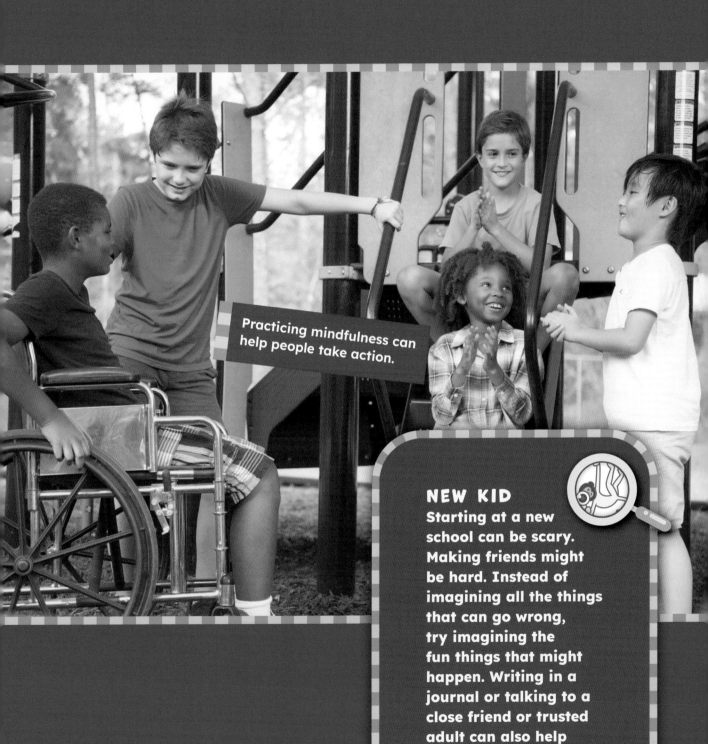

Practicing mindfulness can help people take action.

NEW KID
Starting at a new school can be scary. Making friends might be hard. Instead of imagining all the things that can go wrong, try imagining the fun things that might happen. Writing in a journal or talking to a close friend or trusted adult can also help calm nerves.

Playing with a new group of friends can be fun!

"We're going to play hide-and-seek," Ethan says. "Do you want to join? Cindy is 'it!'"

"Yeah!" Noah says, laughing. He had worried for nothing! Soon, he is playing all kinds of games with his new friends. He is happy he decided to approach them. Practicing mindfulness helped him think about his body and breath. That helped slow down his mind so he could think about the present. Noah was able to put his worries in the background and take action.

WONDER MORE

Wondering about New Information

How much did you know about practicing mindfulness on the playground before reading this book? What new information did you learn? Write down two new facts that this book taught you. Was the new information surprising? Why or why not?

Wondering How It Matters

What is one way mindfulness on the playground relates to your life? If you cannot think of a personal connection, imagine a way it might affect other kids. What impact might it have on their lives?

Wondering Why

Focusing on your body and its reactions is an important part of practicing mindfulness. Why do you think this is important? Do you think it can help you feel calmer when you feel angry or nervous?

Ways to Keep Wondering

Mindfulness can be a complex topic. After reading this book, what questions do you have about it? What can you do to learn more about mindfulness?

TAKING A MINDFULNESS WALK

Being around lots of people on a playground can sometimes feel overwhelming. Taking a mindfulness walk around the playground can help you feel calmer.

1 Figure out a safe walking route. As you walk, focus on each of your senses.

2 First, you can focus on what you see as you walk. What colors do you see the most? Are there clouds in the sky?

3 Then focus on your sense of touch. Are you walking on cement or grass? Is the ground hard? Is it soft?

4 Next, focus on what you hear. Are there loud sounds? Do you hear people talking or playing? Do you hear birds chirping?

5 Finally, focus on smell and taste. Do you smell flowers or grass? Can you taste salt or rain in the air?

GLOSSARY

approach (uh-PROHCH) To approach is to come near someone or something. Noah was glad he decided to approach the kids on the playground.

conflict (KON-flikt) A conflict is a fight. Myla wishes she had acted differently to resolve a conflict with her friend.

focuses (FOH-kuss-iz) When someone focuses, he pays special attention to something. Noah focuses on how his body feels instead of worrying about introducing himself.

forgive (fur-GIV) To forgive someone is to let go of feelings of hurt or anger toward the other person. Myla was able to forgive Jessica, even though Jessica made her mad.

overwhelmed (oh-vur-WELLMD) When thoughts or feelings become too much to handle, a person can feel overwhelmed. Noah felt overwhelmed by fear when he thought of introducing himself to someone new.

regrets (reh-GRETS) Someone who regrets something feels sad or guilty about what happened. Myla regrets her actions toward a former friend.

reject (reh-JEKT) To reject someone or something is to refuse to accept it. Noah is afraid the other kids will reject him.

resolved (reh-ZAHLVD) When a person has resolved something, it means she has found a solution to the problem. Myla thought about the ways she could have resolved her conflict with her friend.

FIND OUT MORE

In the Library

Connors, Kathleen. *Saying I'm Sorry.*
New York, NY: Gareth Stevens, 2015.

Krekelberg, Alyssa. *We Need Each Other: Being a Good Friend.* Parker, CO: The Child's World, 2021.

Verde, Susan. *I Am Love: A Book of Compassion.* New York, NY: Abrams, 2021.

On the Web

Visit our website for links about mindfulness on the playground:

childsworld.com/links

Note to Parents, Caregivers, Teachers, and Librarians: We routinely verify our Web links to make sure they are safe and active sites. So encourage your readers to check them out!

INDEX